The Complete Ketogenic Diet for Beginners:

A Busy Beginner's Guide to Living the Keto Lifestyle with Simple and Easy to Follow Budget Recipes (With Pictures)

By

John R. Kite

Copyright 2017. All rights reserved. No part of this publication may be reproduced, stored in a retrieval system or transmitted in any form or by any means, electronic, mechanical, photocopying, recording or otherwise, without prior permission of the publisher.

Limit of Liability / Disclaimer of Warranty: The publisher and author make no representations or warranties with respect or the accuracy or completeness of these contents and disclaim all warranties such as warranties of fitness of a particular purpose. The author or publisher are not liable for any damages whatsoever. The fact that an individual or organization is referred to in this document as a citation or source of information does not imply that the author or publisher endorses the information that the individual or organization provided.

The information herein is offered for informational purposes only. The presentation of the information is without contract or any type of guarantee assurance. The trademarks that are used are without consent, and the publication of the trademark is without permission or backing by the trademark holder. All trademarks and brands within this book are for clarifying purposes only and are owned by the owners themselves and are not affiliated with this document.

Claim Your Free Gift Now

As a way of saying "thank you" for your purchase, we're offering you a free bonus that's *exclusive* for our book readers.

5 Bonus Instant Ketogenic Diet Recipes!

Go to the link below before it expires!

http://www.easysummaries.com/kdrecipes

The Complete Ketogenic Diet for Beginners

Contents
Claim Your Free Gift Now

The Complete Ketogenic Diet for Beginners:

   Introduction and Overview:

The Complete Ketogenic Diet for Beginners: Benefits

   Body Shape:

   Cholesterol and Sugar Control:

   Mental Capability:

   Cure for Seizures:

   Controlling Blood Pressure:

   Help with Skin Problems:

   Reaching Ketosis:

The Complete Ketogenic Diet for Beginners: Recommended Foods

   Oils and Fats:

   Vegetables:

   Proteins:

   Dairy Items:

   Seeds & Nuts:

Drinks:

The Complete Ketogenic Diet for Beginners: Health issues regarding Ketogenic Diets

Cramps:

Constipation:

Heart Palpitations

Effects on Physical Performance:

The Complete Ketogenic Diet for Beginners: KETOGENIC BREAKFAST RECIPES

Scrambled Eggs

Bacon Veggies Combo

Tofu with Mushrooms

Onion Tofu Scramble

Ham Spinach Ballet

Pepperoni Omelet

Sausage Solo

Creamy ParsleySoufflé

Bacon Bok Choy Samba

Sausage Bacon Beans Cancan

Eggs Stuffed with Avocado & Watercress

Cream Cheese Pancakes

- Watercress Omelet
- Spinach Quiche

The Complete Ketogenic Diet for Beginners: KETOGENIC LUNCH RECIPES

- Air Fried Chicken
- Creamy Chicken Breasts
- Crock Pot Carrots Pork
- Garlic Creamy Beef Steak
- Salmon Stew
- Cheesy Broccoli Soup
- Creamy Chicken Tenders
- KetogenicBeef Sirloin Steak
- Paprika Shrimp
- Bacon Swiss Pork Chops
- Crock Pot Beef Fajitas
- Ketogenic Butter Fish
- Bacon Wrapped Asparagus
- Cheesy Cauliflower

The Complete Ketogenic Diet for Beginners: KETOGENIC DINNER RECIPES

- Shrimp Magic

- Ham Stuffed Veal Rolls
- Jamaican Jerk Pork Roast
- Stuffed Whole Chicken
- Pork Carnitas
- Mexican Taco Casserole
- Sweet and Sour Fish
- Parmesan Roasted Bamboo Sprouts
- Buttered Scallops
- Creamy Turkey Breast
- Cheese Casserole
- CapreseHasselback Chicken
- Mustard Pork Chops
- Buffalo Fish

The Complete Ketogenic Diet for Beginners: KETOGENIC DESSERT RECIPES

- Chocolate Peanut Butter Cups
- Ketogenic Flourless Chocolate Brownies
- Crème Brûlée
- Cream Crepes
- Lemon Mousse
- Nut Porridge

Chocolate Cheese Cake

Mouth-Watering Vanilla Yogurt

Peanut Butter Pudding

Berries Yogurt

Thai Coconut Custard

Ketogenic Avocado Dessert

Peanut Butter Cookies

Ketogenic Cheesecake Cupcakes

The Complete Ketogenic Diet for Beginners' Shopping List:

Dairy and Eggs:

Cheeses:

Meats and Fishes:

Fruits and Vegetables:

Spices:

Oils and Condiments:

Baking Goods:

Sweeteners:

Other Items:

The Complete Ketogenic Diet for Beginners 14-DAY MEAL PLAN JUMP-STARTING YOUR KETOGENIC DIET

Day 1:

Day 2:

Day 3:

Day 4:

Day 5:

Day 6:

Day 7:

Day 8:

Day 9:

Day 10:

Day 11:

Day 12:

Day 13:

Day 14:

The Complete Ketogenic Diet for Beginners: Conclusion

Claim Your Free Gift Now

FINAL SURPRISE BONUS

The Complete Ketogenic Diet for Beginners:

Introduction and Overview:

Some of the combinations of things we eat affect our health significantly. Ketogenic diet has proved to be significant not only for epileptic patients but also has been known to be an effective weight loss method. It stimulates the brain and helps to reduce seizures. It is also high in fat content which contradicts with the common belief that fats are bad for the human body. In this diet, ketones are produced to help the body use fats rather than using glucose to gain energy. In this diet, ketones are produced which help the body to use fats rather than using glucose to gain energy.

Keto diet is not for everyone however, it can be tried. It can be hard to maintain and not everyone's body may be able to cope up with the changes. Try to keep the diet simple and straightforward. Install a tracker on your phone to keep a check on the number of carb consumption. Generally, 70% fat is in this diet whilst only 5% carb intake is there. Don't forget to hydrate as this is a key to stabilize the body. Supplement the diet with a multi-vitamin, this will be helpful in the long run as well. Add milk, nuts, and porridge to breakfast. Adding exercise to this diet will significantly help in the weight reduction. Buying an instant pot and using slow cooker recipes can significantly help with the diet plan. Some side effects of this diet can be cramps, constipation, increased heart beat level and reduced physical performance. In such cases, it is best to seek medical advice and see if any changes can be made to the diet.

The Complete Ketogenic Diet for Beginners: Benefits

Body Shape:

Most people tend to go on this diet because it helps in weight loss. Studies have shown that it is the fastest method of weight reduction than the traditional dieting.

Cholesterol and Sugar Control:

It also helps to decrease cholesterol levels and type-2 diabetes. It has proved to be much an effective method to control sugar.

Mental Capability:

Ketones tend to be a good source of fuel for the mind. Without carbohydrates, there are lesser chances of increments in sugar which help concentration.

Cure for Seizures:

It has proved to be a great source to help reduce seizures especially in children and this can be done alongside minimal medications.

Controlling Blood Pressure:

It is known to help in controlling cholesterol and blood pressure as it helps improve triglyceride levels.

Help with Skin Problems:

A significant difference reduction in acne has been seen in people who try this diet. Excessive amounts of carbs can be a leading cause of skin problems. Ketogenic diet has helped this problem.

Reaching Ketosis:

Reaching ketosis is not a fast process but many people consider ketosis to be the first step in the achieving the benefits of keto diet.

The following steps may be useful in achieving ketosis:

1. **Remove carbohydrates**:

    Ketosis cannot be reached if the body still has glucose in it as a source of providing energy to the body. Carb intake needs to be restricted to 20g or lesser in a day.

2. **Protein Reduction**:

Protein can be slightly risky as eating too much of it might get converted into glucose.

3. Fat increment:

Consumption of healthy fats is important to lose fat on keto so it must be kept in mind that not all fats are bad for health. Feeling hungry all the time will not help weight loss.

4. Hydration:

Water is very important on keto. A lot of consumption of fluids is required. Maintain a record on the amount of water intake and remain consistent. For variety, add some lemon into the water to help you stay hydrated.

5. Healthy Eating:

A caution for a keto diet is that even though while eating the recommended foods, people can still have insulin spikes which may be reduced if snacking is done at a lower level. This will help in weight loss.

6. Intermittent fasting:

Intermittent fasting is recommended while on this diet. This can be done if all meals are eaten within 8 hours instead of spread out throughout the day. This will help in digestion

7. Work out:

A little bit of work-out or a 30 minute walk will help weight loss and help maintain sugar levels. It is to be noted that just because keto gives you more energy does not mean that a marathon can be run.

8. Consider supplements:

Supplements may help reach ketosis earlier however, they are not mandatory. It is important to check the food labels to see what is in it and if sugar is one of the ingredients then avoid it.

The Complete Ketogenic Diet for Beginners: Recommended Foods

Having a diet is not an easy task, especially if a specific meal plan is not provided. The following are some foods which are recommended whilst on this journey. This will help in deciding what to eat and what to shop for. It has been proved that these follow the 5% carbohydrate allowance which is essential for being on a keto diet. In general, the following groups of food are allowed:

Oils and Fats:

Natural resources like mean and nuts are the best way to get healthy fats. This can be substituted and followed by saturated and monosaturated fats like oils from natural resources and butter.

Vegetables:

They can be fresh or from cold storage. It doesn't make much of a difference. But remember to stick towards lefty and ground vegetables.

Proteins:

Always go for meat which has been raised on pastures and grass and is organic in nature. There is no or less added sugar in meats mostly, so it should be ensured that its consumption should be moderate. Excessive protein intake while being on a ketogenic diet is harmful for our health.

Dairy Items:

Whenever buying dairy products, always ensure to buy full-fat dairy products. There are fewer carbohydrates in hard cheese. Many of the dairy items work fine but full-fat are recommended at the most as this is the core of this diet. Some cheeses mostly have little carbohydrates.

Seeds & Nuts:

To keep things interesting, keto dieting people can try nuts however, if someone is allergic to let's assume peanuts, it can be avoided altogether.

Drinks:

Water is highly recommended but it can be supplemented with lemon flavored beverages as well.

The Complete Ketogenic Diet for Beginners: Health issues regarding Ketogenic Diets

There are few complications regarding the intake of ketogenic diets. The most common are the following:

Cramps:

Cramps can be caused due to the lack of magnesium in the body. The most common cramp is the leg cramps which happen on the beginning of starting a ketogenic diets. This usually happens in the mornings or nights and is the result of lacking of minerals like magnesium in the body. Fluid intake and magnesium supplements help in overcoming this issue.

Constipation:

The main reason for constipation is lack of fluid or more commonly known as dehydration. This can be overcome by increasing fluid consumption to almost one gallon per day and with non-starchy vegetables having fibers.

Heart Palpitations

It is also common to note that while converting on ketogenic diet, a person's heart rate is faster and harder than normal. Normally high fluid intake and sufficient salt consumption will overcome the problem, if it doesn't then potassium supplements will help in overcoming the issue.

Effects on Physical Performance:

A person's physical performance may reduce while converting on a ketogenic diet. This is because the body is getting adjusted to using fat for the body needs. Once it gets adjusted, everything will be fine, else cycling carbs before workout may help.

The Complete Ketogenic Diet for Beginners: KETOGENIC BREAKFAST RECIPES

Scrambled Eggs

Serves: 4

Prep Time: 5 minutes

Cooking Time: 8 minutes

Total Time: 13 minutes

Ingredients:

- 8 eggs
- 2 tablespoons butter
- Salt and freshly ground black pepper, to taste

Directions:

1. Whisk together eggs, salt and black pepper in a bowl.

2. Melt butter in a pan over medium-low heat and add the whisked eggs slowly.

3. Stir the eggs continuously in the pan and remove from the heat after 4 minutes.

4. Dish out and serve with browned toasts.

Nutritional Information per Serving:

Calories 151

Total Fat 11.6 g

Saturated Fat 4.6 g

Cholesterol 335 mg

Total Carbs 0.7 g

Sugar 0.7 g

Fiber 0 g

Sodium 144 mg

Potassium 119 mg

Protein 11.1 g

Bacon Veggies Combo

Serves: 4

Prep Time: 5 minutes

Cooking Time: 25 minutes

Total Time: 30 minutes

Ingredients:

- 4 bacon slices
- 1 green bell pepper, seeded and chopped
- ½ cup Parmesan Cheese
- 2 scallions, chopped
- 1 tablespoon mayonnaise

Directions:

1. Preheat the oven to 375degrees F.
2. Grease baking dish with cooking spray.

3. Line the baking dish with bacon slices and top with bell peppers, mayonnaise, scallions and Parmesan Cheese.

4. Bake for 25 minutes and serve alongside a hot cup of tea.

Nutritional Information per Serving:

Calories 197

Total Fat 13.8 g

Saturated Fat 5.8 g

Cholesterol 37 mg

Total Carbs 4.7 g

Sugar 1.9 g

Fiber 0.6 g

Sodium 662 mg

Potassium 184 mg

Protein 14.3 g

Tofu with Mushrooms

Serves: 3

Prep Time: 5 minutes

Cooking Time: 25 minutes

Total Time: 30 minutes

Ingredients:

- 1 block tofu, pressed and cubed into 1-inch pieces
- 1 cup fresh mushrooms, chopped finely
- 4 tablespoons butter
- 4 tablespoons Parmesan cheese, shredded
- Salt and freshly ground black pepper, to taste

Directions:

1. Mix together tofu, salt and black pepper in a bowl.

2. Melt butter in a pan and add the seasoned tofu.

3. Cook for 5 minutes and add mushrooms and Parmesan cheese.

4. Cook for another 5 minutes, stirring occasionally.

5. Dish out and serve with warm tortillas.

Nutritional Information per Serving:

Calories 211

Total Fat 18.5 g

Saturated Fat 11.5 g

Cholesterol 51 mg

Total Carbs 2 g

Sugar 0.5 g

Fiber 0.4 g

Sodium 346 mg

Potassium 93 mg

Protein 11.5 g

Onion Tofu Scramble

Serves: 3

Prep Time: 8 minutes

Cooking Time: 12 minutes

Total Time: 20 minutes

Ingredients:

- 2 blocks tofu, pressed and cubed into 1 inch pieces
- 2 medium onions, sliced
- 2 tablespoons butter
- 1 cup cheddar cheese, grated

- Salt and freshly ground black pepper, to taste

Directions:

1. Mix together tofu, salt and black pepper in a bowl.

2. Heat butter in a pan and add onions.

3. Cook for 3 minutes and add tofu mixture.

4. Cook for 2 minutes and add cheddar cheese.

5. Cover the pan with lid and cook for 5 minutes on low heat.

6. Dish out and serve with whole wheat bread slices.

Nutritional Information per Serving

Calories 184

Total Fat 12.7 g

Saturated Fat 7.3 g

Cholesterol 35 mg

Total Carbs 6.3 g

Sugar 2.7 g

Fiber 1.6 g

Sodium 222 mg

Potassium 174 mg

Protein 12.2 g

Ham Spinach Ballet

Serves: 4

Prep Time: 5 minutes

Cooking Time: 30 minutes

Total Time: 35 minutes

Ingredients:

- 1½ pounds fresh baby spinach
- 8 teaspoons cream
- 14-ounce ham, sliced
- 2 tablespoons unsalted butter, melted
- Salt and freshly ground black pepper, to taste

Directions:

1. Preheat the oven to 360degrees F.
2. Heat butter in a skillet and add spinach.
3. Cook for 3 minutes and drain the liquid completely from the spinach.
4. Grease 4 ramekins with butter and add cooked spinach.
5. Top with ham slices, cream, salt and black pepper.
6. Bake for 25 minutes and dish out to serve hot.

Nutritional Information per Serving:

Calories 188

Total Fat 12.5 g

Saturated Fat 4.4 g

Cholesterol 53 mg

Total Carbs 4.9 g

Sugar 0.3 g

Fiber 2 g

Sodium 1098 mg

Potassium 484 mg

Protein 14.6 g

Pepperoni Omelet

Serves: 4

Prep Time: 5 minutes

Cooking Time: 30 minutes

Total Time: 35 minutes

Ingredients:

- 15 pepperoni slices
- 6 eggs
- 2 tablespoons butter
- 4 tablespoons cream
- Salt and freshly ground black pepper, to taste

Directions:

1. Beat the eggs and stir in the remaining ingredients.

2. Melt butter in a pan and add the egg mixture.

3. Cook for 2 minutes and turn the side.

4. Cook for another 2 minutes and dish out to serve hot.

Nutritional Information per Serving:

Calories 141

Total Fat 11.3 g

Saturated Fat 3.8 g

Cholesterol 181 mg

Total Carbs 0.6 g

Sugar 0.5 g

Fiber 0 g

Sodium 334 mg

Potassium 103 mg

Protein 8.9 g

Sausage Solo

Serves: 4

Prep Time: 5 minutes

Cooking Time: 30 minutes

Total Time: 35 minutes

Ingredients:

- 4 cooked sausages, sliced
- 4 eggs
- 2 tablespoons butter

- ½ cup cream
- ½ cup mozzarella cheese, grated

Directions:

1. Preheat the Air fryer to 360degrees F.

2. Grease 4 ramekins with butter.

3. Mix together cream and eggs in a bowl and beat well.

4. Transfer the egg mixture into ramekins and top with sausage slices and cheese evenly.

5. Place ramekins in Air fryer basket and cook for about 20 minutes.

6. Dish out and serve hot.

Nutritional Information per Serving:

Calories 180

Total Fat 12.7 g

Saturated Fat 4.7 g

Cholesterol 264 mg

Total Carbs 3.9 g

Sugar 1.3 g

Fiber 0.1 g

Sodium 251 mg

Potassium 142 mg

Protein 12.4 g

Creamy Parsley Soufflé

Serves: 1

Prep Time: 5 minutes

Cooking Time: 10 minutes

Total Time: 5 minutes

Ingredients:

- 2 eggs
- 1 fresh red chili pepper, chopped
- 2 tablespoons light cream
- 1 tablespoon fresh parsley, chopped
- Salt, to taste

Directions:

1. Preheat the oven to 390degrees F and grease 2 soufflé dishes.

2. Beat together all the ingredients until well combined.

3. Transfer the mixture into prepared soufflé dishes.

4. Cook for about 6 minutes and dish out to serve immediately.

Nutritional Information per Serving

Calories 108

Total Fat 9 g

Saturated Fat 4.3 g

Cholesterol 180 mg

Total Carbs 1.1 g

Sugar 0.5 g

Fiber 0.1 g

Sodium 146 mg

Potassium 89 mg

Protein 6 g

Bacon Bok Choy Samba

Serves: 3

Prep Time: 5 minutes

Cooking Time: 15 minutes

Total Time: 20 minutes

Ingredients:

- 2 bacon slices
- 4 bokchoy, sliced
- 4 tablespoons cream
- Salt and freshly ground black pepper, to taste
- ½ cup Parmesan cheese, grated

Directions:

1. Season bokchoy with salt and black pepper.

2. Heat oil in a skillet and add bacon slices.

3. Sauté for about 5 minutes and stir in bokchoy and cream.

4. Sauté for about 6 minutes and sprinkle with Parmesan cheese.

5. Cover the lid and cook for 3 minutes on low heat.

6. Dish out and serve with cooked rice.

Nutritional Information per Serving

Calories 112

Total Fat 4.9 g

Saturated Fat 1.9 g

Cholesterol 10 mg

Total Carbs 1.9 g

Sugar 0.8 g

Fiber 0.4 g

Sodium 355 mg

Potassium 101 mg

Protein 3 g

Sausage Bacon Beans Cancan

Serves: 6

Prep Time: 8 minutes

Cooking Time: 7 minutes

Total Time: 15 minutes

Ingredients:

- 6 medium sausages
- 6 bacon slices

- ½ can white beans, boiled
- 1 tablespoon butter
- Salt and freshly ground black pepper, to taste

Directions:

1. Season the sausages with salt and black pepper.

2. Melt the butter in the skillet and add sausages.

3. Cook for 3 minutes and add bacon slices and beans.

4. Cover the lid and allow it to simmer for 3 minutes on low heat.

5. Dish out and serve with whole wheat bread.

Nutritional Information per Serving:

Calories 199

Total Fat 12 g

Saturated Fat 4 g

Cholesterol 32 mg

Total Carbs 9.5 g

Sugar 0.3 g

Fiber 2.3 g

Sodium 538 mg

Potassium 354 mg

Protein 13 g

Eggs Stuffed with Avocado & Watercress

Serves: 6

Prep Time: 10 minutes

Cooking Time: 5 minutes

Total Time: 15 minutes

Ingredients:

- 6 organic eggs, boiled, peeled and cut in half lengthwise

- 1 medium ripe avocado, peeled, pitted and chopped
- 1/3 cup fresh watercress, trimmed
- ½ tablespoon fresh lemon juice
- Salt, to taste

Directions:

1. Arrange a trivet at the bottom of the Instant Pot and add water.

2. Put the watercress on the trivet and close the lid.

3. Set the Instant Pot to "Manual" at high pressure for 3 minutes.

4. Release the pressure quickly and drain the watercress completely.

5. Remove the egg yolks and transfer into a bowl.

6. Add avocado, watercress, lemon juice and salt and mash completely with a fork.

7. Arrange the egg whites in a serving plate and stuff the egg whites with watercress mixture.

Nutritional Information per Serving:

Calories 132

Total Fat 10.9 g

Saturated Fat 2.7 g

Cholesterol 164 mg

Total Carbs 3.3 g

Sugar 0.5 g

Fiber 2.3 g

Sodium 65 mg

Potassium 226 mg

Protein 6.3 g

Cream Cheese Pancakes

Serves: 2

Prep Time: 10 minutes

Cooking Time: 20 minutes

Total Time: 30 minutes

Ingredients:

- 2 organic eggs
- ½ teaspoon ground cinnamon
- 2-ounce cream cheese, softened

- 1 packet stevia

Directions:

1. Put all the ingredients in a blender and pulse till smooth.
1. Keep aside for about 3 minutes and grease a large skillet with cooking spray.
2. Pour ¼ of the mixture and spread it.
3. Cook for about 2 minutes on each side.
4. Repeat with the remaining mixture and serve with whipped cream.

Nutritional Information per Serving:

Calories 163

Total Fat 14.3 g

Saturated Fat 7.6 g

Cholesterol 195 mg

Total Carbs 2.6 g

Sugar 0.4 g

Fiber 0.3 g

Sodium 146 mg

Potassium 95 mg

Protein 6.3 g

Watercress Omelet

Serves: 2

Prep Time: 10 minutes

Cooking Time: 5 minutes

Total Time: 15 minutes

Ingredients:

- 4 large organic eggs, beaten
- 1 cup watercress, chopped
- 2 teaspoons olive oil
- 1 cup cheddar cheese, shredded
- Salt and freshly ground black pepper, to taste

Directions:

1. Heat olive oil in a non-stick skillet and add watercress.

2. Sauté for about 1 minute and add salt and black pepper.

3. Sauté for 30 seconds and transfer the watercress in a bowl.

4. Beat the eggs and add in the same skillet and cook for about 2 minutes.

5. Flip the egg and cook for about 1 minute.

6. Place watercress over half portion of omelet and sprinkle with cheese.

7. Cover the watercress and cheese with the remaining half.

8. Cook for about 1 more minute and cut into 2 wedges.

Nutritional Information per Serving:

Calories 414

Total Fat 33.4 g

Saturated Fat 15.7 g

Cholesterol 431 mg

Total Carbs 1.5 g

Sugar 1.1 g

Fiber 0.2 g

Sodium 502 mg

Potassium 221 mg

Protein 27.2 g

Spinach Quiche

Serves: 5

Prep Time: 10 minutes

Cooking Time: 35 minutes

Total Time: 45 minutes

Ingredients:

- 1 (10-ounce) package frozen spinach, thawed
- 5 organic eggs, beaten
- 1 tablespoon olive oil

- 3 cups Muenster cheese, shredded
- Salt and freshly ground black pepper, to taste

Directions:

1. Preheat the oven to 350degrees F and grease a 9-inch pie dish lightly.

2. Heat olive oil in a large skillet and add spinach.

3. Cook for about 3 minutes and keep aside to cool.

4. Mix together eggs, Muenster cheese, salt, black pepper and cooked spinach.

5. Transfer the mixture into prepared pie dish and bake for about 30 minutes.

6. Remove from the oven and cut into 6 equal sized wedges to serve.

Nutritional Information per Serving:

Calories 349

Total Fat 27.8 g

Saturated Fat 14.8 g

Cholesterol 229 mg

Total Carbs 3.2 g

Sugar 1.3 g

Fiber 1.3 g

Sodium 532 mg

Potassium 466 mg

Protein 23 g

The Complete Ketogenic Diet for Beginners: KETOGENIC LUNCH RECIPES

Air Fried Chicken

Serves: 4

Prep Time: 10 minutes

Cooking Time: 10 minutes

Total Time: 20 minutes

Ingredients:

- 8 skinless, boneless chicken tenderloins
- 2 tablespoons vegetable oil
- 1 teaspoon turmeric powder
- Salt and freshly ground black pepper, to taste

Directions:

1. Season the chicken with salt, black pepper and turmeric powder.
2. Preheat the air fryer to 355°F and coat with vegetableoil.
3. Put the chicken tenderloins in the Air fryer and cook for about 10 minutes.
4. Dish out and serve with mint dip.

Nutritional Information per Serving:

Calories 342

Total Fat 14.9 g

Saturated Fat 4.4 g

Cholesterol 130 mg

Total Carbs 0.4 g

Sugar 0 g

Fiber 0.1 g

Sodium 80 mg

Potassium 14 mg

Protein 50 g

Creamy Chicken Breasts

Serves: 3

Prep Time: 10 minutes

Cooking Time: 15 minutes

Total Time: 25 minutes

Ingredients:

- 1 pound chicken breasts
- 1 small onion
- ½ cup sour cream
- 2tablespoons butter
- Salt, to taste

Directions:

1. Season the chicken breasts with salt and keep aside.

2. Heat butter in a skillet and add onion.

3. Sauté for 3 minutes and add chicken breasts.

4. Cover the lid and cook for 8 minutes.

5. Stir in the sour cream and cook for about 4 minutes.

6. Stir gently and dish out to serve.

Nutritional Information per Serving:

Calories 447

Total Fat 26.9 g

Saturated Fat 12.9 g

Cholesterol 172 mg

Total Carbs 3.8 g

Sugar 1.1 g

Fiber 0.5 g

Sodium 206 mg

Potassium 459 mg

Protein 45.3 g

Crock Pot Carrots Pork

Serves: 3

Prep Time: 10 minutes

Cooking Time: 15 minutes

Total Time: 25 minutes

Ingredients:

- 4 medium carrots, peeled and sliced lengthwise
- 2 pounds pork shoulder roast, boneless
- 1 teaspoon dried oregano, crushed
- 1 large onion, thinly sliced
- Salt and freshly ground black pepper, to taste

Directions:

1. Season the pork shoulder with salt, black pepper and dried oregano.

2. Transfer the pork in a bowl and keep aside for 3 hours.

3. Put carrots and onions in the bottom of a large crock pot and top with the pork shoulder.

4. Set the slow cooker on low and cook for about 8 hours.

5. Dish out and serve with Indian wheat roti.

Nutritional Information per Serving:

Calories 415

Total Fat 30.8 g

Saturated Fat 10.7g

Cholesterol 107 mg

Total Carbs 6.5 g

Sugar 3.1 g

Fiber 1.7 g

Sodium 129 mg

Potassium 171 mg

Protein 26.1 g

Garlic Creamy Beef Steak

Serves: 3

Prep Time: 1 hour

Cooking Time: 30 minutes

Total Time: 1 hour 30 minutes

Ingredients:

- 1 pound beef top sirloin steaks
- 2 garlic cloves, minced
- ¾ cup cream
- ¼ cup butter
- Salt and freshly ground black pepper, to taste

Directions:

1. Rub the beef sirloin steaks with salt, black pepper and garlic.

2. Marinate the beef with butter and cream for 1 hour.

3. Preheat the grill and transfer the steaks on it.

4. Grill for 15 minutes on each side and serve hot with mashed potato.

Nutritional Information per Serving:

Calories 353

Total Fat 24.1 g

Saturated Fat 14.5 g

Cholesterol 113 mg

Total Carbs 3.9 g

Sugar 1.2 g

Fiber 0 g

Sodium 298 mg

Potassium 35 mg

Protein 31.8 g

Salmon Stew

Serves: 3

Prep Time: 5 minutes

Cooking Time: 12 minutes

Total Time: 17 minutes

Ingredients:

- 1 pound salmon fillet, cubed
- 1 medium onion, chopped
- 1 tablespoon butter

- 1 cup homemade fish broth
- Salt and freshly ground black pepper, to taste

Directions:

1. Season the salmon fillets with salt and black pepper.

2. Melt butter in a skillet and add onions.

3. Sauté for about 3 minutes and add salmon.

4. Sauté for about 2 minutes per side and add fish broth.

5. Cover the lid and cook for 6 minutes.

6. Dish out and serve hot with cauliflower rice.

Nutritional Information per Serving:

Calories 272

Total Fat 14.2 g

Saturated Fat 4.1 g

Cholesterol 82 mg

Total Carbs 4.4 g

Sugar 1.9 g

Fiber 1.1 g

Sodium 275 mg

Potassium 635 mg

Protein 32.1 g

Cheesy Broccoli Soup

Serves: 3

Prep Time: 10 minutes

Cooking Time: 4 hours

Total Time: 4 hours 10 minutes

Ingredients:

- 1 cup broccoli

- 1 cup chicken broth

- 1 cup cheddar cheese
- ½ cup heavy whipping cream
- Salt, to taste

Directions:

1. Stir in the broccoli, chicken broth, cheddar cheese, heavy whipping cream and salt in the crock pot.

2. Set the crock pot on low and cook for about 4 hours.

3. Dish out and serve with hot nachos.

Nutritional Information per Serving:

Calories 244

Total Fat 20.4 g

Saturated Fat 67 g

Cholesterol 130 mg

Total Carbs 3.4 g

Sugar 1 g

Fiber 0.8 g

Sodium 506 mg

Potassium 217 mg

Protein 12.3 g

Creamy Chicken Tenders

Serves: 3

Prep Time: 5 minutes

Cooking Time: 20 minutes

Total Time: 25 minutes

Ingredients:

- 1 pound chicken tenders
- 2 tablespoons butter
- ½ cup feta cheese
- ½ cup cream
- Salt and freshly ground black pepper, to taste

Directions:

1. Preheat the oven to 330degrees F.

2. Season chicken tenders with salt and black pepper in a bowl.

3. Melt the butter in a non-stick pan and add chicken tenders.

4. Cook for 5 minutes on both sides and transfer to a baking dish.

5. Top with cream and feta cheese and bake for 15 minutes.

6. Dish out and serve alongside hot cinnamon tea.

Nutritional Information per Serving:

Calories 447

Total Fat 26.4 g

Saturated Fat 13.1 g

Cholesterol 185 mg

Total Carbs 2.3 g

Sugar 1.8 g

Fiber 0 g

Sodium 477 mg

Potassium 400 mg

Protein 47.7 g

Ketogenic Beef Sirloin Steak

Serves: 6

Prep Time: 5 minutes

Cooking Time: 35 minutes

Total Time: 40 minutes

Ingredients:

- 2 pounds beef top sirloin steaks
- 1 teaspoon garlic powder
- 2 garlic cloves, minced

- ¼ cup butter
- Salt and freshly ground black pepper, to taste

Directions:

1. Melt butter in a large grill pan and add beef sirloin steaks.

2. Brown the steaks on both sides by cooking for 2 minutes on each side.

3. Add the remaining ingredients and cook for 15 minutes on each side on medium-high heat.

4. Dish out the juicy steaks in a serving platter and serve with baked potato.

Nutritional Information per Serving:

Calories 246

Total Fat 13.1 g

Saturated Fat 7.6 g

Cholesterol 81 mg

Total Carbs 2 g

Sugar 0.1 g

Fiber 0.1 g

Sodium 224 mg

Potassium 11 mg

Protein 31.3 g

Paprika Shrimp

Serves: 3

Prep Time: 5 minutes

Cooking Time: 20 minutes

Total Time: 25 minutes

Ingredients:

- 1 pound tiger shrimps
- 3 tablespoons butter
- ½ teaspoon smoked paprika

- Salt, to taste

Directions:

1. Preheat the oven to 400degrees F.

2. Mix together all the ingredients in a large bowl.

3. Place the seasoned shrimp in the baking dish.

4. Transfer the baking dish in oven and bake for about 15 minutes.

5. Dish out and serve with red beans dip.

Nutritional Information per Serving:

Calories 173

Total Fat 8.3 g

Saturated Fat 1.3 g

Cholesterol 221 mg

Total Carbs 0.1 g

Sugar 0 g

Fiber 0.1 g

Sodium 332 mg

Potassium 212 mg

Protein 23.8 g

Bacon Swiss Pork Chops

Serves: 4

Prep Time: 5 minutes

Cooking Time: 20 minutes

Total Time: 25 minutes

Ingredients:

- 6 bacon strips, cut in half
- 4 pork chops, bone-in
- 1 tablespoon butter
- ½ cup Swiss cheese, shredded

- Salt and freshly ground black pepper, to taste

Directions:

1. Season the pork chops with salt and pepper.

2. Heat butter in the skillet and add pork chops.

3. Cook for 6 minutes and add bacon strips.

4. Cover the lid and cook for 8 minutes.

5. Sprinkle with cheese and cook for 5 minutes on low heat.

6. Dish out and serve hot.

Nutritional Information per Serving:

Calories 483

Total Fat 40 g

Saturated Fat 16.2 g

Cholesterol 89 mg

Total Carbs 0.7 g

Sugar 0.2 g

Fiber 0 g

Sodium 552 mg

Potassium 286 mg

Protein 27.7 g

Crock Pot Beef Fajitas

Serves: 3

Prep Time: 10 minutes

Cooking Time: 9 hours

Total Time: 9 hours 10 minutes

Ingredients:

- 1 pound beef, sliced
- 1 bell pepper, sliced
- 1 onion, sliced
- 1 tablespoon butter
- 1 tablespoon fajita seasoning

Directions:

1. Put the butter in the bottom of the crock pot.

2. Add beef, onion, bell pepper and fajita seasoning.

3. Set the crock pot on low and cook for about 9 hours.

4. Dish out and serve with egg-fried rice.

Nutritional Information per Serving:

Calories 353

Total Fat 13.4 g

Saturated Fat 6 g

Cholesterol 145 mg

Total Carbs 8.5 g

Sugar 3.6 g

Fiber 1.3 g

Sodium 304 mg

Potassium 738 mg

Protein 46.7 g

Ketogenic Butter Fish

Serves: **3**

Prep Time: **10 minutes**

Cooking Time: **30 minutes**

Total Time: **40 minutes**

Ingredients:

- 1 pound salmon fillets
- 3 green chilies, chopped

- ¾ cup butter
- 2 tablespoons ginger-garlic paste
- Salt and freshly ground black pepper, to taste

Directions:

1. Season the salmon fillets with ginger-garlic paste, salt and black pepper.

2. Place the salmon fillets in the pot and top with the butter and green chilies.

3. Cook on low heat for 30 minutes and serve hot.

Nutritional Information per Serving:

Calories 507

Total Fat 45.9 g

Saturated Fat 22.9 g

Cholesterol 142 mg

Total Carbs 2.4 g

Sugar 0.2 g

Fiber 0.1 g

Sodium 296 mg

Potassium 453 mg

Protein 22.8 g

Bacon Wrapped Asparagus

Serves: 3

Prep Time: 10 minutes

Cooking Time: 20 minutes

Total Time: 30 minutes

Ingredients:

- 6 small spears asparagus
- 2 bacon slices
- 1 tablespoon butter
- ¼ cup heavy whipping cream
- Salt and freshly ground black pepper, to taste

Directions:

1. Season the asparagus spears with salt and black pepper.

2. Add heavy whipping cream to the asparagus.

3. Wrap the asparagus in the bacon slices.

4. Preheat the oven to 360degrees F and grease the baking dish with butter.

5. Put the wrapped asparagus in the baking dish.

6. Bake for 20 minutes and serve immediately.

Nutritional Information per Serving:

Calories 142

Total Fat 12.9 g

Saturated Fat 6.5 g

Cholesterol 38 mg

Total Carbs 1.4 g

Sugar 0.5 g

Fiber 0.5 g

Sodium 324 mg

Potassium 129 mg

Protein 5.5 g

Cheesy Cauliflower

Serves: 3

Prep Time: 10 minutes

Cooking Time: 20 minutes

Total Time: 30 minutes

Ingredients:

- 1 cauliflower head
- ¼ cup butter, cut into small pieces
- 1 teaspoon mayonnaise

- 1 tablespoon prepared mustard
- ½ cup Parmesan cheese, grated

Directions:

1. Preheat the oven to 390degrees F.

2. Mix together mayonnaise and mustard in a bowl.

3. Coat the cauliflower head with the mayonnaise mixture.

4. Arrange cauliflower head in a baking dish and top with butter.

5. Sprinkle with cheese evenly and bake for about 25 minutes.

6. Dish out and serve hot.

Nutritional Information per Serving:

Calories 183

Total Fat 17.2 g

Saturated Fat 10.5 g

Cholesterol 44 mg

Total Carbs 5.5 g

Sugar 2.3 g

Fiber 2.4 g

Sodium 250 mg

Potassium 280 mg

Protein 3.7 g

The Complete Ketogenic Diet for Beginners: KETOGENIC DINNER RECIPES

Shrimp Magic

Serves: 3

Prep Time: 10 minutes

Cooking Time: 15 minutes

Total Time: 25 minutes

Ingredients:

- 1 pound shrimps, peeled and deveined
- ½ teaspoon smoked paprika
- 1 red chili pepper, seeded and chopped
- 2 tablespoons butter
- Lemongrass stalks

Instructions

1. Mix together all the ingredients in a bowl except lemongrass and marinate for about 2 hours.
2. Preheat the oven to 390degrees F.
3. Thread the shrimps onto lemongrass stalks.
4. Bake for about 15 minutes and serve immediately.

Nutritional Information per Serving

Calories 251

Total Fat 10.3 g

Saturated Fat 5.7 g

Cholesterol 339 mg

Total Carbs 3 g

Sugar 0.1 g

Fiber 0.2 g

Sodium 424 mg

Potassium 281 mg

Protein 34.6 g

Ham Stuffed Veal Rolls

Serves: 8

Prep Time: 10 minutes

Cooking Time: 20 minutes

Total Time: 30 minutes

Ingredients:

- 8 (6-ounce) veal cutlets
- 8 ham slices
- 2 tablespoons butter, melted
- 4 tablespoons fresh sage leaves
- Salt and freshly ground black pepper, to taste

Directions:

1. Season the veal cutlets with salt and black pepper.

2. Roll the veal cutlets and wrap each one with ham slices tightly.

3. Coat each roll with butter and place the sage leaves over each cutlet evenly.

4. Heat a non-stick pan and cook for 10 minutes on each side.

5. Dish out and serve with stir-fried vegetables.

Nutritional Information per Serving

Calories 467

Total Fat 24.8 g

Saturated Fat 10 g

Cholesterol 218 mg

Total Carbs 1.7 g

Sugar 0 g

Fiber 0.8 g

Sodium 534 mg

Potassium 645 mg

Protein 56 g

Jamaican Jerk Pork Roast

Serves: 6

Prep Time: 10 minutes

Cooking Time: 25 minutes

Total Time: 35 minutes

Ingredients:

- 2 pounds pork shoulder

- 2 tablespoons butter

- ¼ cup Jamaican jerk spice blend

- ¼ cup beef broth

Directions

1. Season the pork with Jamaican jerk spice blend.

2. Melt the butter in the pot and add seasoned pork.

3. Cook for 5 minutes and add beef broth.

4. Cover the lid and cook for 20 minutes on low heat.

5. Dish out and serve with French fries.

Nutritional Information per Serving

Calories 477

Total Fat 36.2 g

Saturated Fat 14.3 g

Cholesterol 146 mg

Total Carbs 0 g

Sugar 0 g

Fiber 0 g

Sodium 162 mg

Potassium 507 mg

Protein 35.4 g

Stuffed Whole Chicken

Serves: 6

Prep Time: 10 minutes

Cooking Time: 8 hours

Total Time: 8 hours 10 minutes

Ingredients:

- 1 (2-pound) whole chicken, cleaned, pat dried
- 4 whole garlic cloves, peeled
- 2 tablespoons fresh lemon juice

- 1 cup mozzarella cheese
- Salt and freshly ground black pepper, to taste

Directions:

1. Season the chicken with salt and black pepper, and stuff the chicken cavity with garlic cloves and mozzarella cheese.

2. Transfer the chicken in the crock pot and squeeze lemon juice on top.

3. Set the crock-pot on Low, cover and cook for about 8 hours.

4. Dish out and serve with mozzarella sticks.

Nutritional Information per Serving

Calories 309

Total Fat 12.1 g

Saturated Fat 3.6 g

Cholesterol 137 mg

Total Carbs 1.6 g

Sugar 0.7 g

Fiber 0.8 g

Sodium 201 mg

Potassium 390 mg

Protein 45.8 g

Pork Carnitas

Serves: 3

Prep Time: 10 minutes

Cooking Time: 12 minutes

Total Time: 22 minutes

Ingredients:

- 1 pound pork shoulder, bone-in
- 1 orange, juiced
- ½ teaspoon garlic powder

- 1 tablespoon butter
- Salt and freshly ground black pepper, to taste

Directions:

1. Season the pork with salt and black pepper.

2. Put butter in the Instant Pot and select "Sauté".

3. Add garlic powder and sauté for 1 minute.

4. Add seasoned pork in the Instant Pot and sauté for 3 minutes.

5. Stir in orange juice and lock the lid.

6. Set the Instant Pot to "Manual" at High Pressure for 8 minutes.

7. Release the pressure naturally and dish out to serve warm.

Nutritional Information per Serving

Calories 506

Total Fat 36.3 g

Saturated Fat 14.3 g

Cholesterol 146 mg

Total carbs 7.6 g

Sugar 5.8 g

Fiber 1.5 g

Sodium 130 mg

Potassium 615 mg

Protein 35.9 g

Mexican Taco Casserole

Serves: 3

Prep Time: 10 minutes

Cooking Time: 25 minutes

Total Time: 35 minutes

Ingredients:

- 1 pound ground beef
- ½ cup cottage cheese
- 1 tablespoon taco seasoning
- ½ cup cheddar cheese, shredded
- ½ cup salsa

Directions:

1. Mix together the ground beef and the taco seasoning in a bowl.

2. Stir in the salsa, cottage cheese and cheddar cheese.

3. Preheat the oven to 450°F and grease a baking dish.

4. Put the ground beef mixture in the baking dish and top with the cheese mixture.

5. Bake for about 25 minutes and remove from the oven.

6. Serve warm with whole wheat tortilla.

Nutritional Information per Serving:

Calories 409

Total Fat 16.5 g

Saturated Fat 8 g

Cholesterol 158 mg

Total Carbs 5.7 g

Sugar 1.9 g

Fiber 0.6 g

Sodium 769 mg

Potassium 792 mg

Protein 56.4 g

Sweet and Sour Fish

Serves: 3

Prep Time: 10 minutes

Cooking Time: 15 minutes

Total Time: 25 minutes

Ingredients:

- 1 pound fish chunks
- 2 drops liquid stevia
- 1 tablespoon vinegar

- ¼ cup butter
- Salt and freshly ground black pepper, to taste

Directions:

1. Melt the butter in a large skillet and add fish chunks.

2. Cook for 3 minutes and add stevia.

3. Cook for 1 minute and add salt and black pepper.

4. Stir continuously while cooking at medium-low heat for 10 minutes.

5. Dish out in a serving bowl and serve with brown rice.

Nutritional Information per Serving:

Calories 274

Total Fat 15.4 g

Saturated Fat 9.7 g

Cholesterol 54 mg

Total Carbs 2.8 g

Sugar 0 g

Fiber 0 g

Sodium 604 mg

Potassium 8 mg

Protein 33.2 g

Parmesan Roasted Bamboo Sprouts

Serves: 3

Prep Time: 10 minutes

Cooking Time: 15 minutes

Total Time: 25 minutes

Ingredients:

- 1 pound bamboo sprouts
- 2 tablespoons butter
- 1 cup Parmesan cheese, grated
- ¼ teaspoon paprika
- Salt and freshly ground black pepper, to taste

Directions:

1. Preheat the oven at 350degrees F and grease a baking dish.

2. Marinate the green beans with butter, paprika, salt and black pepper, and keep aside for 1 hour.

3. Transfer the seasoned green beans in the greased baking dish.

4. Arrange the baking dish in the oven and bake for 15 minutes.

5. Remove the dish from the oven and serve with ketchup.

Nutritional Information per Serving:

Calories 193

Total Fat 15.8 g

Saturated Fat 10.3 g

Cholesterol 47 mg

Total Carbs 2.1 g

Sugar 0.4 g

Fiber 0.4 g

Sodium 421 mg

Potassium 6 mg

Protein 12.6 g

Buttered Scallops

Serves: 3

Prep Time: 10 minutes

Cooking Time: 15 minutes

Total Time: 25 minutes

Ingredients:

- 1 pound sea scallops
- 2 garlic cloves, minced
- ¼ cup butter

- 2 tablespoons fresh rosemary, chopped
- Salt and freshly ground black pepper, to taste

Directions:

1. Melt butter in a medium skillet on medium-high heat.

2. Add garlic and rosemary and sauté for about 1 minute.

3. Stir in the sea scallops, salt and black pepper and cook for about 2 minutes per side or till properly done.

4. Dish out and serve hot.

Nutritional Information per Serving:

Calories 279

Total Fat 16.8 g

Saturated Fat 10 g

Cholesterol 91 mg

Total Carbs 5.7 g

Sugar 0 g

Fiber 1 g

Sodium 354 mg

Potassium 520 mg

Protein 25.8 g

Creamy Turkey Breast

Serves: 6

Prep Time: 10 minutes

Cooking Time: 15 minutes

Total Time: 25 minutes

Ingredients:

- 1 (2-pound) bone-in turkey breast
- 2 tablespoons butter

- 2 garlic cloves, minced
- 1½ cups Italian dressing
- Salt and freshly ground black pepper, to taste

Directions:

1. Preheat the oven to 325degrees F and grease a baking dish with butter.

2. Mix together minced garlic cloves, salt and black pepper.

3. Rub the turkey breast with the seasoning mixture.

4. Arrange turkey breast in the baking dish and top with Italian dressing evenly

5. Bake for about 2 hours, occasionally coating with pan juices.

6. Dish out and serve warm.

Nutritional Information per Serving:

Calories 369

Total Fat 23.2 g

Saturated Fat 5.1 g

Cholesterol 104 mg

Total Carbs 6.5 g

Sugar 4.9 g

Fiber 0 g

Sodium 990 mg

Potassium 33 mg

Protein 35.4 g

Cheese Casserole

Serves: 3

Prep Time: 15 minutes

Cooking Time: 20 minutes

Total Time: 35 minutes

Ingredients:

- 1 pound sausage scramble
- 5 ounce parmesan, shredded
- 8 ounce mozzarella cheese, shredded
- 8 ounce marinara sauce
- 1 tablespoon olive oil

Directions:

1. Preheat the oven to 375degrees F and grease a baking dish with the olive oil.
2. Place half of the sausage scramble in the baking dish.
3. Spread half of the marinara over the sausage scramble.
4. Top with half of the mozzarella and Parmesan cheese.
5. Layer with the remaining half of the sausage scramble and spread the remaining half of mozzarella and Parmesan cheese.
6. Top with rest of the marinara sauce and bake in the oven for 20 minutes.
7. Dish out and serve with tomato ketchup.

Nutritional Information per Serving:

Calories 521

Total Fat 38.8 g

Saturated Fat 12.8 g

Cholesterol 136 mg

Total Carbs 6 g

Sugar 5.4 g

Fiber 0 g

Sodium 201 mg

Potassium 506 mg

Protein 35.4 g

CapreseHasselback Chicken

Serves: 4

Prep Time: 10 minutes

Cooking Time: 1 hour

Total Time: 1 hour 10 minutes

Ingredients:

- 4 large chicken breasts
- 2 tablespoons butter
- 1 cup fresh mozzarella cheese, thinly sliced
- 2 large roma tomatoes, thinly sliced
- Salt and freshly ground black pepper, to taste

Directions:

1. Make some deep slits in the chicken breasts and rub with salt and black pepper.

2. Stuff the mozzarella cheese slices and tomatoes in the chicken slits.

3. Preheat the oven to 360degrees F and grease the baking tray with the butter.

4. Put the stuffed chicken breasts in the baking tray.

5. Transfer the baking tray in the oven and bake for 1 hour.

6. Dish out and serve hot with yogurt.

Nutritional Information per Serving:

Calories 287

Total Fat 15 g

Saturated Fat 6.6 g

Cholesterol 112 mg

Total Carbs 3.8 g

Sugar 2.4 g

Fiber 1.1 g

Sodium 178 mg

Potassium 473 mg

Protein 33.2 g

Mustard Pork Chops

Serves: 4

Prep Time: 10 minutes

Cooking Time: 9 hours

Total Time: 9 hours 10 minutes

Ingredients:

- 4 pork chops
- 2 tablespoons Dijon mustard
- 1 tablespoon fresh rosemary, coarsely chopped
- 2 tablespoons butter
- Salt and freshly ground black pepper, to taste

Directions:

1. Marinate the pork chops with fresh rosemary, Dijon mustard, salt and black pepper for 2 hours.

2. Put the butter and marinated pork chops in the crock pot.

3. Set the crock pot on low, cover and cook for about 9 hours.

4. Dish out and serve with baked potatoes.

Nutritional Information per Serving:

Calories 315

Total Fat 26.1 g

Saturated Fat 11.2 g

Cholesterol 84 mg

Total Carbs 1 g

Sugar 0.1 g

Fiber 0.6 g

Sodium 186 mg

Potassium 296 mg

Protein 18.4 g

Buffalo Fish

Serves: 3

Prep Time: 10 minutes

Cooking Time: 10 minutes

Total Time: 20 minutes

Ingredients:

- 3 fish fillets
- 1/3 cup Franks red hot sauce
- 1 teaspoon garlic powder
- 3 tablespoons butter
- Salt and freshly ground black pepper, to taste

Directions:

1. Melt the butter in a large skillet and add fish fillets.

2. Cook for 2 minutes on each side and add garlic powder, salt and black pepper.

3. Cook for 1 minute and add Franks red hot sauce.

4. Cover the lid and cook for 5 minutes on low heat.

5. Dish out in a serving platter and serve hot with black beans dip.

Nutritional Information per Serving:

Calories 317

Total Fat 22.7 g

Saturated Fat 9.9 g

Cholesterol 61 mg

Total Carbs 16.4 g

Sugar 0.2 g

Fiber 0.6 g

Sodium 659 mg

Potassium 307 mg

Protein 13.6 g

The Complete Ketogenic Diet for Beginners: KETOGENIC DESSERT RECIPES

Chocolate Peanut Butter Cups

Serves: 5

Prep Time: 10 minutes

Cooking Time: 30 minutes

Total Time: 40 minutes

Ingredients:

- 2 ounces unsweetened chocolate
- ¼ cup heavy cream
- 4 packets stevia
- 1 cup butter

- ¼ cup peanut butter, separated

Directions:

1. Preheat the oven to 360degrees F.

2. Melt the butter and peanut butter in a bowl.

3. Stir intruvia, unsweetened chocolate and heavy cream.

4. Mix thoroughly and put the mixture in a baking mold.

5. Put the baking mold in the oven.

6. Bake for 30 minutes and dish out.

Nutritional Information per Serving:

Calories 479

Total Fat 51.5 g

Saturated Fat 29.7 g

Cholesterol 106 mg

Total Carbs 7.7 g

Sugar 1.4 g

Fiber 2.7 g

Sodium 69 mg

Potassium 193 mg

Protein 5.2 g

Ketogenic Flourless Chocolate Brownies

Serves: 4

Prep Time: 10 minutes

Cooking Time: 10 minutes

Total Time: 40 minutes

Ingredients:

- ½ cup sugar-free chocolate chips

- ½ cup butter
- 1 teaspoon vanilla extract
- 3 eggs
- ¼ cup stevia

Directions:

1. Preheat the oven to 395degrees F and grease a baking mold.

2. Whisk together eggs and add truvia sweetener and vanilla extract.

3. Put the egg mixture in the blender and blend until frothy and light.

4. Put the chocolate and butter in a pan and melt on low heat.

5. Add the melted chocolate mixture the egg mixture.

6. Pour it in the baking mold and arrange the baking mold in the oven.

7. Bake for 30 minutes and dish out to cut into square pieces.

8. You can serve the hot chocolate brownies with whipped cream.

Nutritional Information per Serving:

Calories 266

Total Fat 26.9 g

Saturated Fat 15.8 g

Cholesterol 184 mg

Total Carbs 2.5 g

Sugar 0.4 g

Fiber 0 g

Sodium 218 mg

Potassium 53 mg

Protein 4.5 g

Crème Brûlée

Serves: 4

Prep Time: 10 minutes

Cooking Time: 15 minutes

Total Time: 25 minutes

Ingredients:

- 3 egg yolks

- ½ tablespoon vanilla extract

- ¼ cup stevia
- 1 cup heavy cream
- 1 pinch salt

Directions:

1. Preheat the oven to 365degrees F.

2. Mix together egg yolks, vanilla extract, heavy cream and salt in a bowl and beat until well combined.

3. Divide the mixture evenly into 2 (6-ounce) greased ramekins.

4. Transfer the ramekins in the oven and bake for 15 minutes.

5. Cover the ramekins with a plastic wrap and refrigerate to chill for about 3 hours.

Nutritional Information per Serving:

Calories 149

Total Fat 14.5 g

Saturated Fat 8.1 g

Cholesterol 56 mg

Total Carbs 1.6 g

Sugar 0.3 g

Fiber 0 g

Sodium 56 mg

Potassium 39 mg

Protein 2.6 g

Cream Crepes

Serves: 4

Prep Time: 10 minutes

Cooking Time: 16 minutes

Total Time: 26 minutes

Ingredients:

- 2 tablespoons coconut flour
- 2 organic eggs
- 2 tablespoons coconut oil, melted and divided

- 1/3 cup heavy cream
- 1 teaspoon Splenda

Directions:

1. Mix together 1 tablespoon of coconut oil, eggs, Splenda and salt in a bowl and beat until well combined.

2. Add the coconut flour slowly while continuously beating.

3. Stir in the heavy cream and beat continuously until mixed well.

4. Heat a non-stick pan and pour ¼ of the mixture in it.

5. Cook for 2 minutes on each side and repeat with the remaining mixture in three batches.

6. Serve with additional whipped cream to enhance the taste.

Nutritional Information per Serving:

Calories 145

Total Fat 13.1 g

Saturated Fat 9.1 g

Cholesterol 96 mg

Total Carbs 4 g

Sugar 1.2 g

Fiber 1.5 g

Sodium 35 mg

Potassium 37 mg

Protein 3.5 g

Lemon Mousse

Serves: 4

Prep Time: 10 minutes

Cooking Time: 10 minutes

Total Time: 20 minutes

Ingredients:

- 1 cup heavy cream
- 8-ounces cream cheese, softened
- ¼ cup fresh lemon juice
- 3 pinches salt
- 1 teaspoon lemon liquid stevia

Directions:

1. Preheat the oven to 350 degrees F and grease a ramekin.

2. Mix together heavy cream, cream cheese, fresh lemon juice, salt and lemon liquid stevia in a bowl.

3. Pour in a ramekin and transfer the ramekin into the oven.

4. Bake for 10 minutes and pour into the serving glasses.

5. Refrigerate for at least 2 hours and chill before serving.

Nutritional Information per Serving:

Calories 305

Total Fat 31 g

Saturated Fat 19.5 g

Cholesterol 103 mg

Total Carbs 2.7 g

Sugar 0.5 g

Fiber 0.1 g

Sodium 299 mg

Potassium 109 mg

Protein 5 g

Nut Porridge

Serves: 4

Prep Time: 10 minutes

Cooking Time: 10 minutes

Total Time: 20 minutes

Ingredients:

- 1 cup cashew nuts, raw and unsalted
- 1 cup pecan, halved

- 2 tablespoons stevia
- 4 teaspoons coconut oil, melted
- 2 cups water

Directions:

1. Put the pecans and cashew nuts in the food processor.

2. Pulse until combined and chunked but do not convert into powder form.

3. Transfer the nuts mixture into the pot and stir in coconut oil, wate rand stevia.

4. Cook for 5 minutes on high heat and then reduce the flame.

5. Simmer for 10 minutes on low flame and dish out.

Nutritional Information per Serving:

Calories 260

Total Fat 22.9 g

Saturated Fat 7.3 g

Cholesterol 0 mg

Total Carbs 12.7 g

Sugar 1.8 g

Fiber 1.4 g

Sodium 9 mg

Potassium 209 mg

Protein 5.6 g

Chocolate Cheese Cake

Serves: 3

Prep Time: 10 minutes

Cooking Time: 12 minutes

Total Time: 22 minutes

Ingredients:

- 1 cup cream cheese, softened
- 1 egg

- 1 tablespoon cocoa powder
- ½ teaspoon pure vanilla extract
- ¼ cup swerve

Directions:

1. Preheat the oven to 350 degrees F.

2. Put cream cheese and eggs in an immersion blender and blend until smooth.

3. Pour in the cocoa powder, vanilla extract and swerve.

4. Pulse until well-combined and transfer the mixture into 2 (8-ounce) mason jars evenly.

5. Put the mason jars in the oven and bake for 12 minutes.

6. Refrigerate for at least 5 hours before serving and serve chilled.

Nutritional Information per Serving:

Calories 244

Total Fat 24.8 g

Saturated Fat 15.6 g

Cholesterol 32 mg

Total Carbs 2.1 g

Sugar 0.4 g

Fiber 0.1 g

Sodium 204 mg

Potassium 81 mg

Protein 4 g

Mouth-Watering Vanilla Yogurt

Serves: 4

Prep Time: 20 minutes

Cooking Time: 6 hours

Total Time: 6 hours 20 minutes

Ingredients:

- 2 cups heavy cream
- ½ cup yogurt starter
- ¼ cup stevia

- 1cup full-fat milk

- 1 tablespoon pure vanilla extract

Directions:

1. Pour milk into the crock pot and turn it on low for 3 hours.

2. Whisk in heavy cream, vanilla extract and erythritol and let the yogurt sit.

3. Set the crock pot on low and cook for about 3 hours.

4. Stir in the yogurt starter in 1 cup of milk.

5. Pour this mixture back to the crock pot and whisk it all together.

6. Put the lid back on the crock pot and wrap the entire crock pot in two small towels.

7. Let the wrapped crock pot sit for 9 hours while the yogurt cultures.

8. Dish out in a serving bowl or store it by refrigerating.

Nutritional Information per Serving:

Calories 292

Total Fat 26.2 g

Saturated Fat 16.3 g

Cholesterol 100 mg

Total Carbs 8.2 g

Sugar 6.6 g

Fiber 0 g

Sodium 86 mg

Potassium 250 mg

Protein 5.2 g

Peanut Butter Pudding

Serves: 4

Prep Time: 10 minutes

Cooking Time: 10 minutes

Total Time: 20 minutes

Ingredients:

- 2 cups cashew milk, unsweetened
- 2 teaspoons gelatin
- ½ cup cold water
- 2 tablespoons stevia
- ¼ cup natural peanut butter

Directions:

1. Put unsweetened cashew milk, natural peanut butter and stevia in a bowl and stir well.
2. Heat a cooking pot and pour the mixture in it.
3. Cook for 5 minutes on medium heat.

4. Mix the gelatin in cold water and add to the cooking pot.

5. Stir gently for 5 minutes and let the pudding sit for 1 hour.

6. Pour into 4 serving bowls and refrigerate for 4 hours.

Nutritional Information per Serving:

Calories 124

Total Fat 9 g

Saturated Fat 1.5 g

Cholesterol 0 mg

Total Carbs 4.5 g

Sugar 1 g

Fiber 1 g

Sodium 91 mg

Potassium 13 mg

Protein 8 g

Berries Yogurt

Serves: 4

Prep Time: 20 minutes

Cooking Time: 6 hours

Total Time: 6 hours 20 minutes

Ingredients:

- 2 cups mixed berries
- 2 cups heavy whipping cream
- 3 tablespoons stevia

- 1 small container full fat yogurt

- 3 tablespoons unsweetened gelatin

Directions:

1. Pour heavy whipping cream with some water into the crock pot and turn it on low for 4 hours.

2. Turn off the heat and whisk in gelatin, yogurt, stevia and mixed berries.

3. Set the crock pot on low and cook for about 1 hour.

4. Put the lid back on the crock pot and wrap the entire crock pot in 4 beach towels.

5. Let the wrapped crock pot sit for 10 hours while the yogurt cultures.

6. Dish out in a serving bowl or store it by refrigerating.

Nutritional Information per Serving:

Calories 288

Total Fat 23.1 g

Saturated Fat 14.3 g

Cholesterol 82 mg

Total Carbs 14 g

Sugar 8.4 g

Fiber 2.5 g

Sodium 52 mg

Potassium 136 mg

Protein 6.9 g

Thai Coconut Custard

Serves: 4

Prep Time: 5 minutes

Cooking Time: 25 minutes

Total Time: 30 minutes

Ingredients:

- 1 cup unsweetened coconut milk
- 3 eggs
- 3 packets stevia
- 4 drops vanilla extract

Directions:

1. Put the unsweetened coconut milk in the Instant Pot and select "Sauté".
2. Sauté for 2 minutes and add eggs, erythritol and vanilla extract.
3. Lock the lid and set the Instant Pot to "Manual" at low pressure for 25 minutes.
4. Release the pressure naturally and open the lid.
5. Dish out and chill before serving.

Nutritional Information per Serving:

Calories 197

Total Fat 17.6 g

Saturated Fat 13.7 g

Cholesterol 123 mg

Total Carbs 5.6 g

Sugar 2.8 g

Fiber 1.3 g

Sodium 56 mg

Potassium 208 mg

Protein 5.5 g

Ketogenic Avocado Dessert

Serves: 2

Prep Time: 15 minutes

Cooking Time: 0 minutes

Total Time: 15 minutes

Ingredients:

- 1 ripe avocado, peeled, pitted, and diced
- ½ teaspoon liquid stevia
- ¼ cup heavy whipping cream

- ¼ teaspoon ground cinnamon
- ¼ teaspoon vanilla extract

Directions:

1. Put the avocado in a bowl and mash with the help of a fork.

2. Stir in liquid stevia, heavy whipping cream, ground cinnamon and vanilla extract.

3. Mix thoroughly and refrigerate for at least an hour.

4. Chill before serving and serve in small bowls.

Nutritional Information per Serving:

Calories 259

Total Fat 25.2 g

Saturated Fat 7.6 g

Cholesterol 21 mg

Total Carbs 9.4 g

Sugar 0.6 g

Fiber 6.9 g

Sodium 12 mg

Potassium 501 mg

Protein 2.2 g

Peanut Butter Cookies

Serves: 4

Prep Time: 5 minutes

Cooking Time: 15 minutes

Total Time: 20 minutes

Ingredients:

- 1 cup peanut butter
- 1 teaspoon sugar-free vanilla extract
- ½ cup cream
- ½ cup Swerve

- 1 egg

Directions:

1. Preheat the oven to 350 degrees F and line a baking sheet with parchment paper.

2. Combine peanut butter, cream, egg, Swerve and vanilla extract in a bowl.

3. Mix well until a dough is formed and roll the dough into 1-inch balls.

4. Place on the prepared baking sheet and press down twice with a fork in a criss-cross pattern.

5. Bake in the preheated oven for 14 minutes until the edges are golden.

6. Cool on the baking sheet for 1 minute and transfer to a wire rack to cool completely before serving.

Nutritional Information per Serving:

Calories 415

Total Fat 35.2 g

Saturated Fat 8.2 g

Cholesterol 47 mg

Total Carbs 14 g

Sugar 6.7 g

Fiber 3.8 g

Sodium 321 mg

Potassium 444 mg

Protein 17.8 g

Ketogenic Cheesecake Cupcakes

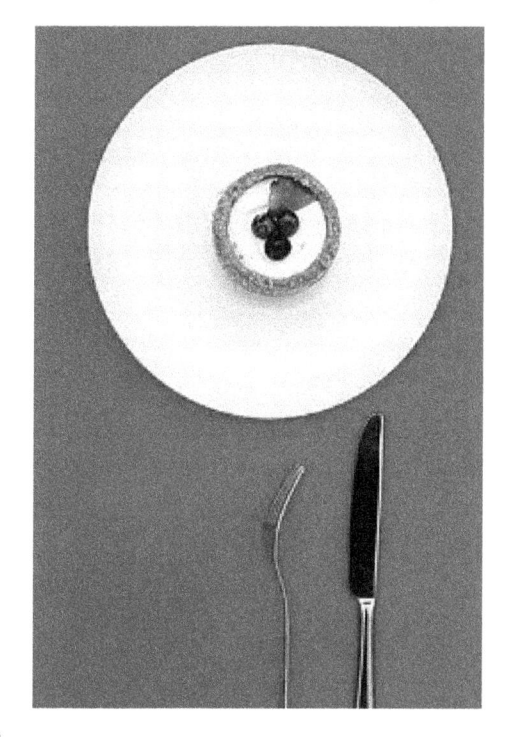

Serves: 4

Prep Time: 10 minutes

Cooking Time: 17 minutes

Total Time: 27 minutes

Ingredients:

- ¼ cup almond meal
- 1(8 ounce) package cream cheese, softened

- 3 tablespoons butter, melted
- ½ cup erythritol
- 1 egg

Directions:

1. Preheat the oven to 350 degrees F and line 6 muffin cups with paper liners.

2. Mix butter and almond meal together in a bowl and spoon into the bottoms of the paper liners.

3. Press the mixture into a flat crust.

4. Put egg, cream cheese and erythritol in a bowl and beat with an electric mixer set to medium until smooth.

5. Spoon over the crust layer in the paper liners.

6. Bake in the preheated oven for 17 minutes until the cream cheese mixture is nearly set in the center.

Nutritional Information per Serving:

Calories 324

Total Fat 32.5 g

Saturated Fat 18.5 g

Cholesterol 126 mg

Total Carbs 3.1 g

Sugar 0.5 g

Fiber 0.7 g

Sodium 245 mg

Potassium 128 mg

Protein 7 g

The Complete Ketogenic Diet for Beginners' Shopping List:

Dairy and Eggs:

5 dozen eggs

4½ pounds butter

4½ pounds heavy whipping cream

½ pound sour cream

1 gallon milk (full fat)

1 pound yogurt (full fat)

1 pound cashew milk (unsweetened)

Cheeses:

1½ pounds parmesan cheese

2 pounds cheddar cheese

3 pounds mozzarella cheese

2 pounds cream cheese

1½ pounds Muenster cheese

½ pound feta cheese

½ pound Swiss cheese

½ pound cottage cheese

1½ pounds parmesan cheese

Meats and Fishes:

Chicken:

½ pound chicken broth

2 pounds chicken breasts

6 pounds chicken tenders loins (bone in)

2 pounds whole chicken (cleaned)

Beef:

1 pound beef (ground)

1 pound beef

½ pound beef broth

3 pounds beef sirloin steaks

8 veal cutlets (6 oz each)

Pork:

8 pork chops (bone in)

3 pounds pork shoulders (bone in)

40 oz Ham

8 bacon slices

6 bacon strips

8 Ham slices

2 pounds pork

14 bacon slices

6 bacon strips

Seafood:

1 pound sea scallops

2 pounds fish chunks

1 pound sea scallops

2 pounds salmon fillets

1 pound fish broths

1 pound shrimps

2 pounds tiger shrimps

Others:

6 pounds Turkey Breast (bone in)

2½ pounds sausages (medium)

Fruits and Vegetables:

½ pound scallions

½ pound mushrooms

1 pound onions

2 pounds spinach

½ pound parsley

1 pound spear asparagus

1 pound bokchoy

½ pound carrots

1 pound broccoli

2 pounds watercress

1 pound cauliflower head

½ pound sage leaves

1 pound bamboo sprout

½ pound tomatoes

½ pound avocados

1 pound rosemary

½ pound garlic

½ pound lemongrass stalks

Spices:

1 pound Salt

1 pound Black pepper

½ pound green chili

½ pound green bell pepper

1 pound pepperoni slices

½ pound red chili pepper

½ pound cinnamon

½ pound turmeric powder

½ pound derived oregano

½ pound smoked paprika

½ pound bell pepper

½ pound taco seasoning

½ pound Fajita seasoning

½ pound Jamaican jerk spice blend

Oils and Condiments:

½ pound olive oil

½ pound salsa

½ pound Dijon mustard

½ pound mustard

½ pound lemons (for juice)

1 pound Italian dressing

½ pound vinegar

½ pound coconut oil

½ pound mayonnaise

Baking Goods:

1 pound vanilla extract

1 pound coconut floor

½ pound sugar free chocolate chips

½ pound chocolate (sugar free)

½ pound coco floor

½ pound cocoa powder

½ pound coco milk

Sweeteners:

8 packets stevia

2 liquid stevia

1 packet Splenda

Other Items:

3 blocks tofu

½ pound red beans (canned)

½ pound gelatin

1 pound peanut butter

½ pound almond meal

The Complete Ketogenic Diet for Beginners 14-DAY MEAL PLAN JUMP-STARTING YOUR KETOGENIC DIET

If you are a ketogenic diet beginner, then you must follow this 14-day meal plan. This meal plan comprises of daily breakfast, lunch, dinner and dessert recipes. As a beginner, you must follow this 14-day meal plan which will definitely help you lose inches off your waist.

Day 1:

Breakfast: Scrambled Eggs
Lunch: Air Fried Chicken
Dinner: Shrimp Magic

Dessert: Chocolate Peanut Butter Cups

Day 2:

Breakfast: Spinach Quiche
Lunch: Cheesy Cauliflower
Dinner: Buffalo Fish
Dessert: Ketogenic Cheesecake Cupcakes

Day 3:

Breakfast: Bacon Veggies Combo
Lunch: Creamy Chicken Breasts
Dinner: Ham Stuffed Veal Rolls
Dessert: Ketogenic Flourless Chocolate Brownies

Day 4:

Breakfast: Watercress Omelet

Lunch: Bacon Wrapped Asparagus

Dinner: Mustard Pork Chops

Dessert: Peanut Butter Cookies

Day 5:

Breakfast: Tofu with Mushrooms
Lunch: Crock Pot Carrots Pork
Dinner: Jamaican Jerk Pork Roast
Dessert: Crème Brûlée

Day 6:

Breakfast: Cream Cheese Pancakes
Lunch: Ketogenic Butter Fish
Dinner: CapreseHasselback Chicken
Dessert: Ketogenic Avocado Dessert

Day 7:

Breakfast: Onion Tofu Scramble
Lunch: Garlic Creamy Beef Steak
Dinner: Stuffed Whole Chicken
Dessert: Cream Crepes

Day 8:

Breakfast: Eggs Stuffed with Avocado & Watercress
Lunch: Crock Pot Beef Fajitas
Dinner: Cheese Casserole
Dessert: Thai Coconut Custard

Day 9:

Breakfast: Ham Spinach Ballet
Lunch: Salmon Stew
Dinner: Pork Carnitas
Dessert: Lemon Mousse

Day 10:

Breakfast: Sausage Bacon Beans Cancan
Lunch: Bacon Swiss Pork Chops
Dinner: Creamy Turkey Breast
Dessert: Berries Yogurt

Day 11:

Breakfast: Pepperoni Omelet
Lunch: Cheesy Broccoli Soup
Dinner: Mexican Taco Casserole
Dessert: Nut Porridge

Day 12:

Breakfast: Bacon Bok Choy Samba
Lunch: Paprika Shrimp
Dinner: Buttered Scallops
Dessert: Peanut Butter Pudding

Day 13:

Breakfast: Sausage Solo
Lunch: Creamy Chicken Tenders
Dinner: Sweet and Sour Fish
Dessert: Chocolate Cheese Cake

Day 14:

Breakfast: Creamy Parsley Soufflé
Lunch: Ketogenic Beef Sirloin Steak
Dinner: Parmesan Roasted Bamboo Sprouts
Dessert: Mouth-Watering Vanilla Yogurt

The Complete Ketogenic Diet for Beginners: Conclusion

Food deprivation can be fatal for any living body. But the type of food we eat defines our health in its own significant way. The ketogenic diet has low carbohydrates and higher fats and is the ultimate key in weight loss. The process of ketosis aids in maintaining the physical shape of our body and alongside it provides us with a nutritious diet. Apart from its medical uses like for the cure of seizures, cholesterol level controlling, blood pressure controlling, mental health improvement, and skincare etc. the ketogenic food is easy to convert on unlike vegetarian diets.

To have a successful ketogenic life style one should reduce the intake of carbohydrates. Improve fat consumption, reduce proteins and remain hydrated. The diet plan should be calculated prior to converting on the ketogenic to avoid any hardships. The ketogenic diet plan is easy to follow and have meals from almost every food category and for every occasion. A wide range of healthy and delicious breakfasts, lunches, dinners, snacks and desserts can be prepared using ketogenic recipes. In case of medical complication like crabs or constipation etc. one should immediately consult a physician for expert opinion for any alterations to the diet plan.

Claim Your Free Gift Now

As a way of saying "thank you" for your purchase, we're offering you a free special bonus that's *exclusive* for our book readers.

5 Bonus Ketogenic Diet Recipes!

Go to the link below before it expires!

http://www.easysummaries.com/kdrecipes

FINAL SURPRISE BONUS

Final words from the author…

Hope you enjoyed this book as much as we enjoyed bringing it to you!

I always like to over-deliver, so I'd like to give you one final bonus.

Do me a favor, if you enjoyed this book, please leave a review.

It will help get the word out so more readers can enjoy this book!

If you do, I'll send you one of my most cherished collection – Free:

5 More Tantalizing Recipes on The Complete Ketogenic Diet for Beginners: A Busy Beginner's Guide to Living the Keto Lifestyle with Simple and Easy to Follow Budget Recipes (With Pictures) By John R. Kite!

Here's how to claim your free report:

1. Leave a review (longer the better but I'd be grateful for whatever length)

2. Send a screenshot of the review here: easysummaries24@gmail.com

3. Receive your bonus within 24-48 hours!

Receive your free bonus – 5 More Tantalizing Recipes on **The Complete Ketogenic Diet for Beginners: A Busy Beginner's Guide to Living the Keto Lifestyle with Simple and Easy to Follow Budget Recipes (With Pictures) By John R. Kite!** – *immediately*!

CPSIA information can be obtained
at www.ICGtesting.com
Printed in the USA
LVHW02s0020040918
589084LV00002B/75/P